for C —

stay true!

NATION OF LAWYERS

by Paul Williams

illustrated by Donna Nassar

Entwhistle Books

Glen Ellen

11/90

Thanks to Dan Joy, Robert Lichtman,
Raymond Mungo, Tim Underwood.

6 5 4 3 2 1

1st printing, June 1990
ISBN 0-934558-15-9

Available from your bookstore or from:

Entwhistle Books
Box 611
Glen Ellen, CA 95442 USA

CONTENTS

Nation of Lawyers   1

Silence and Rage   31

How to Tell the Truth   39

The Awakening   49

Right to Pass   57

appendix   112

NATION OF LAWYERS

We must quit now
this nation of lawyers.

Without criticizing or condemning
what we leave behind,
let us open our arms
to a life based on trust
in the spirit, not the letter,
of the Law.

Let us do what we can
— and what we have to —
to take money down
a peg or two
from its place of importance
in our lives.

You are not what you buy.
You are not what you get paid.

Remembering this,
you'll find it a lot easier
not to be for sale.

What can we do
to improve our world?

We can take apart the lie machine.

This is not just a job
for those who have lived
in authoritarian nations.

It is also a job for all who live
in media nations,

corporate takeover nations,

banker nations,

nations of advertisers,

nations of bureaucrats,

nations of senators,

nations of lawyers.

Take apart the lie machine.

Not only in the world around you
but most of all
in your own daily life.

Unplug the sucker.

Speak from your heart.

Be truthful, be loving.
Be gentle, be firm.
Be radical, be courageous.

Be yourself.

It sounds so simple.
It's not.

Because in the name of the self
our worst lies are spoken.

Our great enemy
is self-importance.

It keeps us apart
when we could be together.

It keeps us proud and confused
when we could be asking for guidance.

It keeps us angry
when we could forgive.

Nation of lawyers
doesn't get paid for forgiveness.

Nation of advertisers
can't afford higher guidance.

Nation of journalists
knows only too well
it's easier to sell fear
than love.

Today we transform ourselves.

Today the wall of fear and control
  comes down.

Today the passageway of courage and risk
  is opened.

And we don't know where it leads.

Today we renounce our materialism.
Today we take our eyes off the prize
and let go.

Today we begin to trust
that this really is the great adventure
we always wanted it to be.

The adventure requires courage.
Courage means heart.

When you have the courage of your convictions,
you are following the path of your heart.

Do not pledge yourself.

To swear yourself to any group, any organization,
any idea, is to cut yourself off from spirit,
from the living voice of your heart.

Keep your path open.

Trust your heart.

Don't let "commitments"
take the place of convictions.

Be honest.
Be present.
Be modest and courageous.

Spirit will take care of the rest.

Do not pledge yourself to another person.

Only give yourself.

But be aware that by your giving
you are accepting this person
as a mirror in your life
now and always
reflecting back the truth
about who you have become.

If you keep this awareness
you won't give yourself lightly.

You may think of this giving as a pledge, if you like,
but remember
it means nothing
unless you renew it
through your actions
apart and together
over and over and over again
here in each present moment of your lives.

You are not alone.

Loneliness is the price of self-importance.

It is cured by reaching out to the one who is always with you — Allah, Jesus, Goddess, Buddah, spirit, companion, higher self, the universe, namelessness, whatever you do or don't call it — and asking for guidance and support.

You don't have to ask in words.

Just open up a space of listening.

When you remember that you're not alone,
you can give yourself to another person
and there will be something there to give.

This is not religion.

This is just truth.

Truth is expressed in practice.

It is not to be believed.

It is to be lived.

Live your truth
and the lie machine will turn to rust
all over this planet.

We are building something —
growing into something —
quite extraordinary.

The lawyers and politicians and journalists
can't stop us.

But they can distract us, if we let them.

They can slow us down.

We must be careful where we put our attention.

Beware of the con artists, the doom-sayers, and the
  positive thinkers.

Bad news and good news are one and the same:
  a product for someone to sell, and a stimulus
  to the purchase of other products.

Don't be distracted.

We are here to notice,
          to feel,
          to respond,
          to breathe,
          to heal
          and to love.

This planet is wounded.

Let us neither deny nor despair.

Our loving, honest, unflinching attention
    to the wounds
    may or may not bring the healing we long for.

But the only question worth asking is,
    is my heart in the work?

If your heart's not in the work,
   don't argue with it.

Listen to what it tells you.

It will bring you to what you have to do.

We are building something.

We don't have to know what it is.

Today we transform ourselves.

Without criticizing or condemning
what we leave behind,
let us open our arms
to a life based on trust
in the spirit, not the letter,
of the Law.

SILENCE AND RAGE

Silence and rage
are opposite expressions
of the same feeling.

Only by breaking through the silence
can you dissipate the rage.

Only by getting in touch with your rage
can you find the key
to unlock the silence.

There is reason for rage.

Rage is the violent, incoherent expression
of the unexpressible.

It is silence at its loudest.

But it is still silence.

Break the cycle.

Break the cycle of mistrust
with trust.

Break the cycle of silence
by speaking your heart's truth.

Break the cycle of fear
with courage.

Take a risk.

Risk is action.

Action implies responsibility.

That is what we are most afraid of.

Take a deep breath.

Forgive your enemies.

Count your blessings.

Go on living.

HOW TO TELL THE TRUTH

When you just *have* to talk,
   try being silent.

When you feel reluctant to say anything,
   make the effort
   to put what you're feeling into words.

This is a place to begin.

Pushing gently
against the current
of your own impulses
is an effective technique
for dislodging
and discovering
your truth.

How to tell the truth?

Taste it
and remember the taste in your heart.

Risk it
from the bottom of your love.

Take the risk
of telling the truth
about what you're feeling.

Take the risk
of telling your loved one
your secrets.

It's true
you might be misunderstood.

Look and see
if you're willing to trust
yourselves
to misunderstand each other
and go on from there.

"Understanding
can only be created
out of misunderstanding."
A great man once told me that.
I still don't know if it's true.
But the truth that's in it
has nourished me for decades.

When someone speaks to you
and you feel yourself not wanting to hear it
try letting it in.
You don't have to agree that they're right.
Just take the risk
of listening
as if they could possibly be speaking some truth —
and see what happens.

Listen as if.
Listen as if you can't always tell
what the truth is.
Listen as if you might be wrong,
especially when you know you're right.
Listen as if
you were willing to take the risk
of growing beyond
your righteousness.

Listen as if
love mattered.

THE AWAKENING

The awakening did not occur
twenty years ago
or two thousand years ago.

Take it down off that altar
and smash it to pieces.

It is occurring now
or not at all.

The awakening is happening now.

This is your personal invitation
to take part in the festivities.

You may not get another chance.

The awakening will not be televised.

You have to go down to the street
and meet it in person.

If you've forgotten how to do that,
    don't worry.

When awakening arrives, a door opens;
and everything we need to remember
rushes to us
from behind that door.

Trust the process.

Why? Why should you trust the process?

Because it is your secret creation.
Because it is the living expression of God's will
And because I asked you to.

And because, if you don't trust it, you'll never know
what might have happened if.

There is no specific path to awakening.

There is no way of knowing
what you'll do once you're awake.

Your trust, therefore, must be large indeed.

This is the gift you can give.

RIGHT TO PASS

note:

This is not for those
to whom hate comes easily.

Their task
as they know too well
is to learn to love.

They (whoever they may be)
need our help.
This is not for them.

This is for those traitors
who wish to surrender
and go over to the other side
that the two may be one again.

Politicians shouldn't hold office.

There's a war going on.

A successful business is one that
loses money.

Get it straight.

People like to be scared.

(Roller coaster.
Costs a quarter.)

God bless the people who fight the power plants.

Learn to hate.

Nobody knows what's going on in my mind but me.

And me, I'm struggling to stay afloat here. The more simply and directly I speak, the more mysterious my words become. What sort of a book is this? It is a demand, a colossal demand.

Learn to hate.
Learn what it means
to love so much
that you feel yourself hating everything
that seems to come between you
and your love.

You are
fucking
everyone
you know.

have some respect

love/ when you can
love/ whenever you can

hate/ when you can
hate/ whenever you can

respect your opponent
or you are a
    dead man

good news! good news!
you are making love with
every person
    man
    woman
    tree
    pet
    child
you come in
     contact
    with...

you bastard
you're fucking us all

I hate you

I love you

At any given moment
that I feel something
        for you

I am trying
to tell the secret

Ladies and men
won't you come out
tonight?

Come on out
for some love
or a fight.

I want it all.

I want the sky and the mountains,
the trees and the rocks and the goats
and the oceans.

I want the men and the women
and the children.

I want the moon and the sun and
the stars.

I want to be loved.

I want it all; but I ask
   only the right to pass.

It's a colossal demand.

Politicians shouldn't hold office;
they should dance on the head of a pin

I'm a politician.

I'm a politician, which is to say
an actor, writer, reporter, ambassador-
at-large, TV commentator, composer,
economist, charlatan, fool: in a word,
a mediator.

I'm in the middle of things.

I represent every thing and every
one that I'm aware of.

May I know you?

All I ask is your support;
all I promise is that I will
    accept it.

There's a war going on.

(That's what politicians always say.)

There's a war going on between
women and men.

Man.

Woman.

Each has something the other wants.

Each stands for something the other detests.

Attraction/repulsion.
It's an energy-generating struggle.

Male/female is the key to the source
of the force.

I am a man.

A successful business should be
  losing money.

Spread it around.

Spend.

God bless the people who fight the power plants.

God help the traitors who dare
   love each other.

There's a war going on.

Get it straight.

Get it straight.

Get it straight.

Get it straight.

Get it straight.

appendix: The Story of "Right to Pass"

Raymond Mungo and I were walking in a redwood
forest in Little River, California, Thanksgiving Day
1971, when we found the following sign, large black
letters on white cloth, stapled to a tree:

NOTICE

RIGHT TO PASS IS
BY PERMISSION ONLY
AND SUBJECT TO
CONTROL BY OWNER
Civil Code Section 1008

Boise Cascade Corp.

I removed the sign from the tree and stuffed it in
my pocket. I understood pretty well what the Boise
Cascade Corporation was trying to tell me — they
didn't mind if I walked in their woods this time, but
they wanted it to be on record that I did so only by
their express permission, and that that permission
could be revoked at any time.
I hated the sign and what it stood for; but I liked it

too, because it defined so precisely the issue at stake in the never-ending conflict between the likes of me and the likes of "Boise Cascade Corp." The issue is the right to pass. I know I've got it; they believe they've purchased it. I want to exercise it; they want to control it. They have all the power of the Law and the State on their side, except for one little loophole: precedent. The Law (in California, anyway) recognizes continual use of land as a precedent that cannot legally be denied: for example, if I've been getting to my cabin (or if the previous occupants have) for twenty years on a road that crosses your land, you can't close that road, even though it's your private property. I used to live on a bit of California property that drew its water from a spring on the adjoining property, which happened to be lumber company land. The lumber company had allowed the owner of this property to get her water from that spring back in the nineteen-thirties; subsequent owners had used the spring as their water source ever since, and now the lumber company was forbidden to deny such use, or to foul or destroy the spring. Undoubtedly, frustrating situations like this had resulted in the printing of the "right to pass" signs — to make sure that no such precedents were established in times to come.

What the lumber company (which is what Boise Cascade is) and all other "Corp."s and property nolders fail to realize is that me and my kind have

113

been living on and using this planet continuously for millions of years. We've been getting food, water, shelter, air, and light from this environment unceasingly throughout our stay here, and our right to do so cannot be abridged — neither directly, by controlling our freedom of movement, nor indirectly by fouling or destroying the resources we depend on.

I hold this truth to be self-evident. However, since the "Corp." saw the need to put up a sign, I thought it would be a good idea if we put out a pamphlet of our own, something to put the other side on notice, a response. The resulting fifty-two page essay was written in a notebook in December 1971, mostly in the town of Lund, British Columbia; it was then published in a green passport-sized booklet (first printing, 500 copies) by a Chinese printer in Bangkok, Thailand, in May 1972, under the supervision of Raymond Mungo. About sixty copies of the book were distributed in Asia; the rest were shipped by slow boat back to the United States.

This book is dedicated

to my children's children

Other books by the same author:

Outlaw Blues
Pushing Upward
Time Between
Das Energi
Apple Bay, or Life on the Planet
Coming
The Book of Houses (with Robert Cole)
The International Bill of Human Rights (editor)
Common Sense
Waking Up Together
Only Apparently Real: The World of Philip K. Dick
Remember Your Essence
The Map
Performing Artist: The Music of Bob Dylan
Heart of Gold